Fact Finders®

Kids' Guide to Government

UNDERSTANDING YOUR CIVIL RIGHTS

By Emma Carlson Berne

Consultant: Margo Schlanger
Director of Civil Rights Litigation Clearinghouse
University of Michigan Law School

CAPSTONE PRESS
a capstone imprint

Fact Finders Books are published by Capstone Press,
1710 Roe Crest Drive, North Mankato, Minnesota 56003
www.mycapstone.com

Library of Congress Cataloging-in-Publication Data
Names: Berne, Emma Carlson, author.
Title: Understanding your civil rights / by Emma Carlson Berne.
Description: North Mankato, Minnesota : Capstone Press, [2018] | Series:
Kids' guide to government
Identifiers: LCCN 2017046887 (print) | LCCN 2017047981 (ebook) |
ISBN 9781543503272 (eBook PDF) | ISBN 9781543503357 (reflowable Epub) |
ISBN 9781543503197 (library binding) | ISBN 9781543503234 (paperback)
Subjects: LCSH: Civil rights—United States—Juvenile literature. |
United States. Constitution 1st–10th Amendments—Juvenile literature. Classification:
LCC KF4749 (ebook) | LCC KF4749 .B465 2018 (print) |
DDC 342.7308/5—dc23
LC record available at https://lccn.loc.gov/2017046887

Editorial Credits
Michelle Hasselius, editor; Mackenzie Lopez, designer;
Jo Miller, media researcher; Kathy McColley, production specialist

Photo Credits
AP Images, 11; Getty Images: Archive Photos/Robert Abbott Sengstacke/Contributor,
19, Bettmann/Contributor, 15, 21, The LIFE Images Collection/Carl Iwasaki, 13;
Newscom: Icon SMI/Chris Keane, 5, Sipa USA USA/Hahn Lionel, 17, White House
via CNP/Pete Souza, 12; Shutterstock: ciud, 22, elenabsl, 6-7, hvostik, 24, Kdonmuang,
28, Mascha Tace, 27, Monkey
Business Images, 25, Rob Marmion, cover, Ste studio, 23, Steven Frame, 14, stock_
photo_world, 26

Design Elements
Capstone

Printed and bound in Canada.
010801S18

TABLE OF CONTENTS

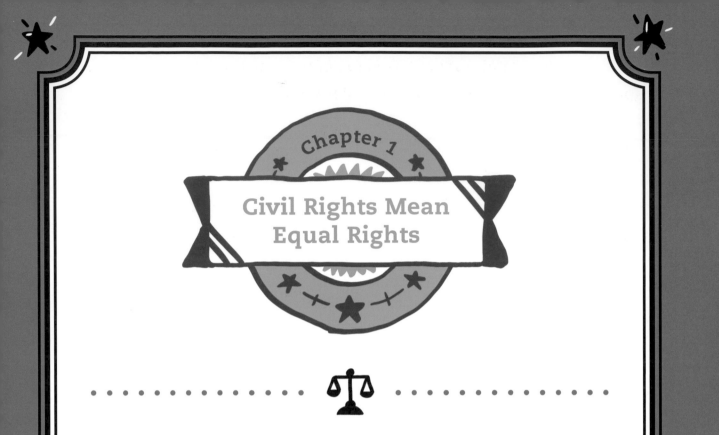

Chapter 1

Civil Rights Mean Equal Rights

"I never expected to be treated so badly because of who I am."
—Coral Aviles

In 2010 a 13-year-old student named Coral Aviles wore a Mexico soccer jersey to school. She wanted to support the country in the World Cup, an international soccer competition. Coral said that a teacher asked her if she was Mexican. When Coral said yes, the teacher asked why Coral was in the United States — in front of the entire class.

The middle-school student talked to her principal about what happened. The principal removed Coral from the class for the rest of the school year.

Coral believes she was **discriminated** against because of her race. With the help of the Mexican American Legal Defense and Education Fund (MALDEF), Coral and her mother filed a federal lawsuit against the school district. Their lawyers plan to prove that the school and the teacher **violated** Coral's civil rights.

Fans cheered for Mexico during the World Cup on March 24, 2010.

discriminate—to treat a person or group unequally, often because of race, religion, gender, sexual preference, or age
violate—to break a rule or a law

What Are Civil Rights?

Civil rights are the rights of all people to be treated equally under the law. These rights protect people from being discriminated against because of their gender, race, religion, age, disability, religion, or nationality. One of the most important jobs our government has is to protect the rights of its citizens. Elected representatives pass laws that establish civil rights for all Americans.

FACT

The words "civil rights" come from the Latin words *ius civis*, which mean rights of a citizen.

The Justice System and Civil Rights

Civil rights violations are often brought before the court system for review. A person or group might **sue** a government body, a business, or a school over a civil rights issue. Judges can order these organizations to change their policies if they are breaking the law.

FACT

The National Association for the Advancement of Colored People (NAACP) is an organization that works to protect a person or group's civil rights and eliminate racial discrimination. The NAACP is the country's oldest and largest civil rights organization. It was founded in 1909.

sue—to bring a suit or case against someone in a court of law

Chapter 2

The 14th Amendment: Civil Rights Superstar

The 14th amendment to the U.S. Constitution guarantees that people in this country have the right to be treated equally and fairly. It states that the government cannot pass laws that discriminate or treat people unfairly. The government must protect the rights of all people who live here.

So what is the problem? Despite this amendment, groups of people have not been treated equally in the United States. People have had to fight for their civil rights at different points throughout this country's history. Some are still fighting today.

Some Civil Rights Events in America

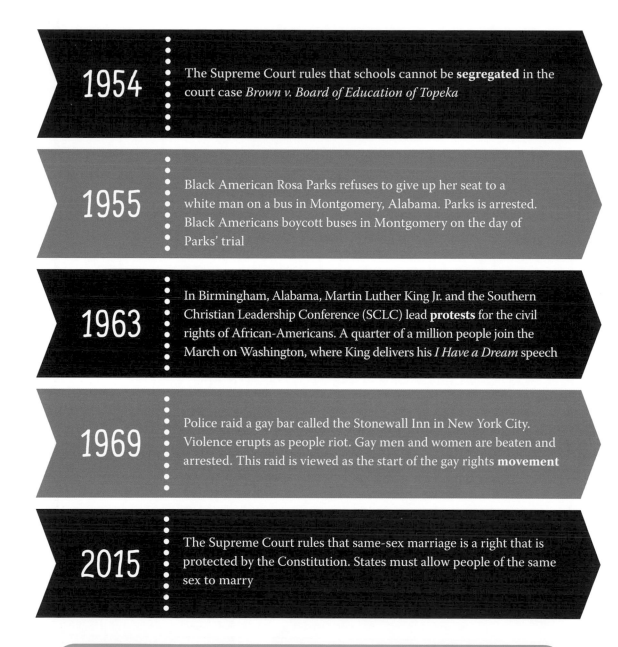

1954
The Supreme Court rules that schools cannot be **segregated** in the court case *Brown v. Board of Education of Topeka*

1955
Black American Rosa Parks refuses to give up her seat to a white man on a bus in Montgomery, Alabama. Parks is arrested. Black Americans boycott buses in Montgomery on the day of Parks' trial

1963
In Birmingham, Alabama, Martin Luther King Jr. and the Southern Christian Leadership Conference (SCLC) lead **protests** for the civil rights of African-Americans. A quarter of a million people join the March on Washington, where King delivers his *I Have a Dream* speech

1969
Police raid a gay bar called the Stonewall Inn in New York City. Violence erupts as people riot. Gay men and women are beaten and arrested. This raid is viewed as the start of the gay rights **movement**

2015
The Supreme Court rules that same-sex marriage is a right that is protected by the Constitution. States must allow people of the same sex to marry

segregate—to keep people of different races apart in schools and other public places
protest—to speak out about something strongly and publicly
movement—a group of people who supports a cause

"There were barricades and people shouting and policemen everywhere. . . . As we walked through the crowd, I didn't see any faces. I guess that's because I wasn't very tall and I was surrounded by the marshals. People yelled and threw things. I could see the school building and it looked bigger and nicer than my old school. When we climbed the high steps to the front door, there were policemen in uniforms at the top. The policemen at the door and the crowd behind us made me think this was an important place."

—*Through My Eyes*, by Ruby Bridges

On November 14, 1960, Ruby Bridges became the first black student to attend an all-white elementary school in the South. She was only six years old. Ruby's parents pushed to let Ruby attend the school. William Frantz Elementary School was much closer to Ruby's house than the all-black school miles away. Her parents also thought she would receive a better education there. A judge ordered the school to accept Ruby as a student.

U.S. marshals walked with Ruby as she left school in November 1960.

FACT

In 1954 the Supreme Court had ruled that black and white children could no longer be separated in school in *Brown v. the Board of Education of Topeka.*

Fifty years after Ruby Bridges walked into William Frantz Elementary School, she was invited to meet President Barack Obama at the White House. Together they looked at a famous picture that hung outside of the Oval Office. It's a portrait of Ruby walking into school. The painting is *The Problem We All Live With*, by Norman Rockwell.

"I think it's fair to say that if it wasn't for you guys, I wouldn't be here today."
—President Obama to Ruby Bridges

Ruby Bridges stood with President Obama in front of Rockwell's painting of her at the White House.

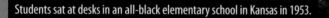

Students sat at desks in an all-black elementary school in Kansas in 1953.

Segregated Schools

Before 1954 public schools in the South were segregated. This meant that black and white children could not go to school together. Schools for black students were supposed to be as good as schools for white students, but they weren't. Most black schools were not given the same amount of money or supplies for their students.

Affirmative Action and Civil Rights

In 1973 Allan Bakke applied to medical school at the University of California, Davis. Bakke had good grades and scored well on the MCAT, the medical school admission exam. But he was rejected from the school twice. Bakke believed he was denied because of his race — he is white. The school could only take a certain number of students each year. According to the school's **affirmative action** program, several spots were reserved for students from different **minority** groups. Bakke wasn't allowed in, even though his grades and test scores were higher than some of the students who had been accepted. Bakke believed his civil rights had been violated. Others supported the university's affirmative action program. They argued that the school's policies were necessary to protect the rights of minority students.

Bakke sued the school. Eventually the U.S. Supreme Court heard the case. On June 28, 1978, Bakke won his case and was admitted to the university's medical school. Bakke became a doctor. Since Bakke's case, the Supreme Court has ruled that affirmative action is allowed. However, it must be flexible and should be part of a process that carefully considers all differences among potential students.

Allan Bakke on his first day of medical school after he won his Supreme Court case

FACT

Some people were angry about the Supreme Court's decision. More than 1,500 students protested. They held signs and marched from the White House to the Capitol building in Washington, D.C.

affirmative action—an active effort to improve the educational and employment opportunities of members of minority groups and women
minority—group of people of a particular race, ethnic group, or religion living among a larger group of a different race, ethnic group, or religion

Chapter 3

Civil Rights Protests: Then and Now

People in the United States still protest for their civil rights today. In 2012 a civil rights movement called Black Lives Matter was founded. The movement promotes awareness of racism against black Americans. Thousands of people have marched and protested to spread this message. By peacefully protesting, this group has linked itself to those who protested earlier, among them the people who fought for African-American **equality** during the 1950s and 1960s.

Other groups have also protested for equality in this country. For example, more than 1 million people in the United States participated in the Women's March on January 21, 2017. This massive protest was held to protect women's reproductive rights, to end violence against women, and to protect human rights. In all, nearly 5 million people marched around the world.

People protested in front of the White House during the Women's March in Washington, D.C.

FACT

In 2017 Black Lives Matter won the Sydney Peace Prize from the Sydney Peace Foundation in Australia. The award is given to a person or group who promotes peace around the world.

equality—being equal, especially in status, rights, and opportunities

Civil Rights Laws

Many minority groups have achieved significant victories throughout the years. Several civil rights laws have been passed. But the struggle continues.

1964 — Congress passes the Civil Rights Act, which forbids discrimination in jobs, schools, stores, restaurants, and hotels based on a person's race, religion, gender, or origin

1965 — The Voting Rights Act of 1965 prohibits discrimination by election officials against voters based on their race

1967 — The Age Discrimination in Employment Act is passed. Employers cannot discriminate against people who are 40 years old or older

1968 — The Fair Housing Act protects people from discrimination during the sale, rental, and financing of housing based on race, religion, or gender

1975 — The Individuals with Disabilities Education Act is passed. This requires public schools to provide education to kids with disabilities

1978 — The Pregnancy Discrimination Act is passed, which prohibits discrimination based on pregnancy and childbirth

1990 — Congress passes the Americans with Disabilities Act (ADA). The ADA protects people against discrimination based on their disabilities

Protesters marched for civil rights in Chicago in 1965.

Nonviolent Protests

The civil rights movement is remembered for using nonviolent protests. Civil rights leader Martin Luther King Jr. encouraged protesters to not fight back if they were attacked. They used peaceful methods to make their points. King was not the first person to use this type of protest. He learned about **civil disobedience** by studying **philosophers** such as Henry David Thoreau. King also learned about Mohandas Gandhi, the leader of the movement for Indian independence during the 1930s and 1940s. Gandhi was among the first to use nonviolent marches and protests in the 20th century.

civil disobedience—refusal to obey government commands, especially as a nonviolent way of forcing preferred action from the government
philosopher—a person who studies ideas, the way people think, and the search for knowledge

Chapter 4

You Have Rights Too

When you're a kid, other people have a say in what you can and cannot do. Parents and teachers have rules that you must follow at home and at school. But your rights are protected under the Constitution, just like adults' rights. For example, you cannot be discriminated against at school because of your race or the religion you practice.

You also have other rights, such as the right to free speech. There have been many debates about what children can say and write in school.

For instance, you cannot write threatening messages about other students on social media. This rule protects other students from online bullying and dangerous speech. But not all student speech can be limited at school.

In December 1965 students Mary Beth Tinker and her brother John wore black armbands to school to protest the Vietnam War. They were asked to remove their armbands. The students refused and were suspended.

The Tinkers sued the school district. The Supreme Court ruled that schools could not limit a student's free speech unless it kept other students from learning. The Tinkers won the case.

Mary Beth and John held up the black armbands they wore to protest the Vietnam War.

What You Can Do

"For the first time this year, I feel like I can actually make it through my senior year of high school just like any other boy in my class. . . . I'm so relieved I'll be able to just go to class, apply to college, and graduate without worrying if I'll get in trouble for using the restroom."
—Ashton Whitaker

Ashton "Ash" Whitaker is a **transgender** boy from Kenosha, Wisconsin. When a person is transgender, that person is thought to be one gender at birth, based on physical appearance. However, the person identifies as another gender.

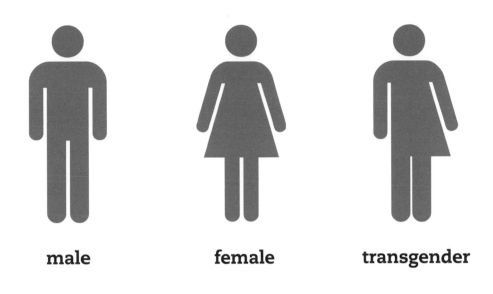

male   female   transgender

Ash wanted to use the boys' restroom at his high school. But Ash's school told him that he had to use the girls' restroom. He could also use a bathroom for both boys and girls in the school's office.

Ash was angry. He felt that he was not receiving the same treatment as other students in his school. He felt that his civil rights were being violated. Ash was 16 years old when his family sued the school district. In 2016 his family won the case. A federal district court ruled that Ash must be allowed to use the boys' restroom. The next year a federal appeals court agreed. Ash hopes his case will help other transgender children who are fighting for equality.

transgender—a person who identifies with a gender that is different from the one assigned at birth

Standing up at School

Imagine you are at school and notice a Muslim student being bullied in the hallways because of the religion he or she practices. Or you see that people who use wheelchairs are struggling to enter your community center because there are no handicapped-accessible doors. These are examples of discrimination.

There are many ways to bring awareness of civil rights issues to your school or community. Here is what you can do if you see someone being treated unfairly.

Talk to a parent or teacher. Discuss what you saw and why you think it was wrong. Brainstorm ways to fix it.

Write a letter to your school principal. In your letter, say exactly what you noticed.

Get other students involved. Sign your letter and ask as many other students as you can to sign it too.

Ask for action. Give the letter to the principal and ask him or her to take action.

Standing up in Your Community

If you see discrimination in your community, speak up at the next city council meeting. At these meetings, leaders of city government get together and make decisions for the community. Most city council meetings are open to everyone — even kids! There's usually a time when the public can speak during the meeting.

Citizens spoke at public hearing at Austin City Hall in Austin, Texas.

Find out when and where the next city council meeting is. Ask your parents to take you. Write an explanation of the discrimination you've seen and what you want the city to do to change it. Read loudly and clearly and get ready to answer questions.

You could also talk to your parents about organizing a peaceful protest. Make signs stating your position. Then tell others who feel the same way to make signs as well. Be ready to explain your position if anyone asks.

Protest Letter

No matter how you choose to get involved, be proud of speaking up for yourself and others. Our civil rights are written into the very foundation of our country. Now it's up to all of us to protect them.

If you see unfair treatment at school or in your community, writing a letter of protest can be a powerful statement. This will help you get started.

[Add the date.],

[Include the name of the person or group you are writing to.]____

[Add the person or group's street address.]____

[City, State, and Zip Code]____

Dear ____,

My name is _____. I attend _____ School and am _____

years old. I am writing to protest the treatment of_____. Since

____[date]_____, I have noticed _____[Write a description of what you have

noticed. Make sure to include a lot of details.]

I do not think this treatment is fair. I propose that the _____[school or community

group]_____ should consider these actions to address this discrimination:

[Solution 1]_____

[Solution 2]_____

[Solution 3]____

Please let me know how you plan to address this situation.

Thank you.

Sincerely,

[Sign your name in pen.]

[Print or type your name.]

    [Write your address.]

Glossary

affirmative action (uh-FUR-muh-tiv AK-shuhn)—an active effort to improve the educational and employment opportunities of members of minority groups and women

civil disobedience (SI-vil diss-uh-BEE-dee-uhnss)—refusal to obey government commands, especially as a nonviolent way of forcing preferred action from the government

discriminate (dis-KRI-muh-nayt)—to treat a person or group unequally, often because of race, religion, gender, sexual preference, or age

equality (i-KWAH-luh-tee)—being equal, especially in status, rights, and opportunities

minority (mye-NOR-uh-tee)—group of people of a particular race, ethnic group, or religion living among a larger group of a different race, ethnic group, or religion

movement (MOOV-muhnt)—a group of people who supports a cause

philosopher (fuh-LOSS-uh-fer)—a person who studies ideas, the way people think, and the search for knowledge

protest (PRO-test)—to speak out about something strongly and publicly

segregate (SEG-ruh-gate)—to keep people of different races apart in schools and other public places

sue (SOO)—to start a suit or case against someone in a court of law

transgender (transs-JEHN-dur)—a person who identifies with a gender that is different from the one assigned at birth

violate (VYE-uh-late)—to break a rule or a law

Critical Thinking Questions

1. Ruby Bridges attended the William Franz Elementary School in 1960. Why was this important?

2. Minority groups have protested for their civil rights. What does "minority" mean?

3. Describe two ways you can make your community aware of a civil rights issue. Use the text to help you with your answer.

Read More

Braun, Eric. *Taking Action for Civil and Political Rights.* Who's Changing the World? Minneapolis: Lerner Publications, 2017.

Levinson, Cynthia. *The Youngest Marcher: The Story of Faye Hendricks, a Young Civil Rights Activist.* New York: Atheneum Books for Young Readers, 2017.

Schwartz, Heather E. *The Civil Rights Act of 1964: A Primary Source Exploration of the Landmark Legislation.* We Shall Overcome. North Mankato, Minn.: Capstone Press, 2015.

Internet Sites

Use FactHound to find Internet sites related to this book.

Visit *www.facthound.com.*

Just type in 9781543503197 and go.

Super-cool stuff! Check out projects, games and lots more at **www.capstonekids.com**

Index